What Is Consciousness?

Regina Leffers, Ph.D.

Enjoy!

Regina

DEDICATION

I have had a daily practice of meditation for going on forty years now. It isn't any particular brand of meditation, although I've tried many different methods. About thirty years ago, I had an experience that affected me profoundly. I wrote it down and have kept it where I could read it once in a while. The page it is written on is yellowed and ragged-edged.

> I entered into a space—it seemed like a room, but there were no boundaries. It felt populated by presences, and then as I just stayed with the experience, it felt more like a single Presence. The whole feeling in the room was that of total, focused, intense interest. I felt as though this Presence couldn't wait to see what I would choose to do next! Presence was completely absorbed by the unfolding of me in particular, as when one is completely taken up in a book such that it is impossible to put the book down—the story **has you**—it holds your interest completely. As I continued the meditation with unwavering attention, I began to experience this Presence holding that same level of intense interest in

Humanity. I experienced the attention of
this Presence absolutely riveted upon us. I
felt no judgment, only care and excited
interest.

When I first experienced this meditation, I didn't quite
know what to make of it. And to tell the truth, it kind of
scared me. But as I've continued to work with it, I have
experienced more of this Presence's interest, sometimes
even as I go about the business of living my everyday life.
In more recent years, I have come to know that my life—
what I choose to do with each moment—best mirrors the
quality of this Presence when I am completely absorbed, or
even dissolved in what I am doing. I experience no
separation between me, the material with which I am
working, and the action I am taking.

This book is dedicated to that Presence.

CONTENTS

ACKNOWLEDGMENTS

I want to thank the members of the Focus Group for this book, who met with me weekly for almost half a year. They have lent their intelligence and tenacity to this project, and in the process, we've all learned more about consciousness.

Thank you Ann Beeching, Beth Murphy Beams, Ellen Sauer, Calvin Sauer, and Cheryl Spieth Gardner for meeting with me in person every week. I want to thank you especially for the work we did together to discuss and discard existing models of consciousness, and come up with and hash through new models, until we finally landed on one that accurately represents the way in which we grow in consciousness.

Calvin, thank you especially for the word "facet," which changed everything!

And thank you Pat Oppor, Gina Sanders, and John Beams for reading the material and either talking with me in person, or calling, emailing, or texting comments and suggestions to me.

I am filled with gratitude for your contributions.

Thanks, with all my heart,

Reg

INTRODUCTION

My intention in writing this book is to create an exploration in consciousness. In my experience, books written about consciousness are written in academic language making them inaccessible to anyone who isn't primarily a student of psychology or neuroscience. The topic is important enough that every person should have access to this body of knowledge. It's something we all experience—every single one of us. For that reason, we should all get a good idea about where we've come from, where we're headed, and where we are right now.

I use my own experience as examples of the different facets of consciousness in the hope that you will be able to think about them in your own experience and relate to them. If you do, you will be able to use it to recognize when a part of you feels stuck and assist yourself in the process of growing yourself through the pain of being stuck. If you don't know where you've been and have no idea where you're going, it's very difficult to know where you are, right? It's simply a guessing game inside of a landscape crapshoot if there's no map to refer to. This material is important enough that it ought to be included in every high school and college psychology course.

I am working from these Truths:

- o Consciousness is experienced *in the body*; it is not just an intellectual concept.

- o We can accept ourselves as we were/are/will be, in all of our imperfections.

- o Loving ourselves wholeheartedly is one of the single most important tasks we have to accomplish in life. This sets the interior stage for us to be able to love others wholeheartedly.

- o Staying open and vulnerable is also one of the single most important tasks we have to accomplish in life.

- o When we live these truths, the experience of compassion—for ourselves, for others—will be one of the natural outcomes. The experience of inner peace will be another.

We move into and through facets of consciousness as we respond to different life conditions, which have unique problems that need to be solved. Each facet is developmentally important in its own right. In order for us to be healthy human beings, each facet is essential for us to grow into, learn how to solve the problems we encounter, and take those skills and strengths with us in other areas of life.

Problems can occur for both self and society when we are stuck in any given facet of consciousness.

If we are stuck in one facet, we may be rationalizing a situation to ourselves to try to maintain the status quo, or we may not have the insight needed to see our way out of a problematic situation. This condition of being stuck is painful. In order for us to overcome the existing barrier, we may have to do something uncomfortable. I'll give examples of this in the following chapters, but just briefly, the uncomfortable action we may need to take almost always requires that we face a fear.

If closed in a facet of consciousness, we are literally blocked from movement. The pain we experience is usually acute. The condition of being absolutely unable to move could be caused by an earlier traumatic psychological experience. It might also be caused by anything that renders us incapable of being able to recognize a barrier for what it is. If we can't recognize it, we can't overcome it. People who are terrified of change can be imprisoned in living life from the inside of one facet of consciousness forever.

If we find ourselves feeling pain, stuck and unable to move, we can gain insight from doing internal work, like therapy, journaling, or meditation, or from a life jolt, like losing a job or being in a car accident. The insight we gain must be large enough to cause a critical level of internal psychological dissonance that essentially wakes us up and urges us to take action.

This book is divided into four sections. In the first section we'll talk about consciousness and discuss how we grow. Old models are linear and hierarchical—they talk about consciousness in terms of stages or layers that can't accurately describe the way consciousness grows in us. All facets are essential to our own development as individual human beings, and to the development and growth of the consciousness of the larger group/society to which we belong. It would be nice to think that the growth happens in a very neat, stepwise progression, right? We'll talk about what really happens in chapter two.

The second section holds the next six chapters and covers the initial six facets of consciousness. I use examples from my own experience to help explain each facet, and talk about what it might look and feel like to be stuck there. By using examples from my own life, I am hoping that you will be able to identify facets expressed in your life, as well as areas in which you may be stuck.

The third section describes the last three facets of consciousness of which we are currently aware. The *Be Creation* facet is the most expanded stage of consciousness that has been identified to this point in our human story.

The fourth section of this book, the Appendix, provides some guidance for getting unstuck. The pain we experience in life can be directly correlated to being stuck in a facet of consciousness that no longer works to address the demands of our living conditions.

And the last bit you should read about consciousness in this Introduction is that in each facet, and in every area of life *we make a choice to live from love or to live from fear* at any given moment in time. Because of that, each chapter on the individual facets begins with a statement about what love is and what fear is when experienced from the inside of that facet. This may become a powerful rubric for you to use in your exploration of consciousness, *especially if you develop the ability to feel love and fear in the body.*

Section One

The fundamentals, questions and answers/proposals:

What is consciousness?

How do we grow in consciousness?

What is the shape of consciousness?

WHAT IS CONSCIOUSNESS?

Imagine consciousness as a cloud of potential awareness, part of the unseen world that permeates all of the space and material of existence. We are born as, into, and with that potentiality.

When we are conscious, we are awake and aware of our surroundings. We are aware of or perceiving something, and we are aware *that we are aware* of both our own mind and of the world in which we are immersed. As I write this, I know that I am both thinking about the material and writing it. As you read this, you are aware that you are both thinking about the material and reading.

Every single morning, we wake up. Sometimes when we awaken, it feels like we come to the surface in stages. Other times it happens abruptly. We were asleep; now we're awake. Eyes open up. We become aware of the body and how it feels. We may have a remnant of a dream hanging out in the mind. We notice the bedroom, the feeling of the floor underfoot, the temperature of the air, the degree of lightness in the sky. We become awake and aware of our surroundings.

We can lose consciousness in more ways than by simply going to sleep. If we're concussed in an accident, are "put under" by an anesthesiologist during an operation, or faint for some reason, we lose consciousness. We can also lose it by using a substance like drugs, alcohol, or even sugar that causes the loss. When we "come to", that is, when we become awake and aware of ourselves and of our surroundings, it happens in much the same way as it does when we awaken from sleep.

Our ability to be conscious, awake and aware of our surroundings can also be affected by any addictions we have, any well-worn path we've walked (metaphorically speaking), and any enculturated ideas that we unwittingly try to live. What this means is that we may be conscious (awake) in some parts of life and unconscious (asleep) in others.

When it comes to addiction affecting my ability to be

awake and aware, I'm thinking here of Girl Scout Thin Mint cookies. I mean really! I cannot have those cookies in my house. After I ate an entire box all by myself, in one sitting, I realized I might have a problem. When I told a friend about the experience, she recommended I store the cookies in the freezer and take just a couple of cookies out at one time. Right. Like that would stop me from inhaling a sleeve of Thin Mints! Ha! I discovered they're even better direct from the freezer, and the entire box disappears just as fast! No! Faster! My consciousness disappears into a sugar-induced haze. The same thing happens with peanut M&M's. I simply cannot buy them! Ever!

The metaphoric well-worn path that I'm referring to is any habitual thoughts or feelings we have. At the end of the day, life is made of the sum total of our thoughts, feelings, and the actions we've taken because of them. And lots of those thoughts and feelings and the resulting actions are completely unconscious, habitual choices we're making.

I just experienced a feeling this morning that can be used to illustrate this. As I listened to the song "Unchained Melody," I experienced an overwhelming feeling of unrequited and lost love. This song was popular when I was a teenager, when feeling bereft and unloved was a dramatic weekly event. That feeling from long ago flooded my emotions as I listened. Luckily, I caught myself in the act. I noticed the habitual and unconscious nature of the feeling and stopped myself. My conscious self knows that I am thoroughly loved, and that there is always enough love to go around. I want my life to be built from the conscious understanding of the caveat that there is always enough love, and that if we let it, it permeates everything.

Another example of a habitual, metaphoric well-worn path from my own experience has to do with my reaction to a former friend when he insisted that he was right, and being right was the most important thing to him. I may not have even had any skin in the game, that is, I may have simply exclaimed something like: "What a gorgeous day!" And in response, he might tell me that I'm wrong about that because it's going to rain shortly. So, while I was saying something about what the day feels like inside of me, he would take it as a literal statement about the weather.

My unconscious response to his interpretation was to feel instantly angry. It was completely unconscious. For a time, I loaded the feeling of anger with an also unconscious story line or thought process that went something like this: "He squashes my enthusiasm every time I express it. Argh! It feels like he's trying to control me!"

He is a literal guy and has spent an adult lifetime doing work in which his ability to be literal determined his level of success in his work. I am pretty sure that I was born enthusiastic. My working edge in that scenario was to wake up to the feeling of anger when it ramped up inside of me, to stop the habitual story response before it started, and to allow the angry feeling to dissolve. I would remind myself that his literal interpretation had nothing to do with me.

A final example of this has to do with my own unconscious thoughts and feelings about my body. We are all good and tired of thinking there is something wrong with the shape of our bodies, right? If you've read my last book, *I Am A Miracle Magnet*, you know all about my own struggle with this, so I won't repeat it here. If you haven't read it, just look at your own feelings about your body — you know — the ones that live in the dark corners of life experience — the ones that criticize abs, thighs, ankles, bellies, breasts or chest, or any body part at all, really.

I am working consciously to both stop and replace negative thoughts and feelings about my body. Every morning when I meditate and every day when I walk, I set the intention for a joyful, energetic, and vital body. I am cultivating feelings of gratitude for my strength and endurance and shape. After all, we human beings come in all shapes and sizes. There is simply no one, single shape and size that is the measure of health or beauty. And that brings us to the next way in which we can be asleep in pieces of our consciousness: enculturated rules about right and wrong ways to behave.

Just as we've been taught, often subliminally, that there is only one beautiful or handsome shape for a person, other ideas and rules about culturally approved ways to be have been passed on to us as well. In his excellent book, _The Code of the Extraordinary Mind_, (which I highly recommend), Vishen Lakhiani coins a new word to describe the unquestioned, enculturated rules that we follow. He calls them "Brules," which is short for bullshit rules. Following them effectively prevents us from living our lives authentically.

One example of an enculturated rule is about acceptable careers for women and men. When I was in grade school, I remember our eighth-grade teacher asking class members what career they wanted to pursue. Every girl responded with one of the following professions: nun, wife and mother, teacher, nurse, or the possibility, at that time brand new, for girl's vocations, stewardess. (And we all knew, of course, that a stewardess would have to be blond, thin, and beautiful to be hired to do the work.) This was in 1962. There was no name for what I wanted to do—not inside of me, and not outside of me. I probably said "nun" at the time.

That was a long time ago, and you might be thinking that a lot has changed regarding career opportunities for women and men since I was in grade school, and I agree that possibilities have expanded for both genders. After all, there are now women who are doctors and engineers, and men who are nurses and interior designers. But doing just a thin skiff of research on current career stats for women and men will uncover cultural expectations still firmly held in place.

It took me some time to figure out what I wanted to be when I grew up because of these enculturated limits. On my website, I state that I am a "midwife to the birth of the Wild Soul," and that is a pretty good description of what I want to be in the world. The act of writing this book is an example of me doing what I enjoy doing. I love to think about the place in which Psychology and Philosophy intersect.

It has taken me a long time to learn to be what I want to be in the world, to be conscious, awake and alive, in this area of life. The process of getting here has been interesting, exciting, and oftentimes hard. I am hoping that as you read this book, you will be able to identify places in life in which you are following a grooved, enculturated, and perhaps an inauthentic road, bring it to the surface, and make conscious choices, more truly reflective of your own "wild soul," your authentic core self.

One Action to Take Today to Explore Consciousness:

Pick one activity you do each day that is normally automatic, like breathing, eating a meal, or working out at the gym, and consciously choose to stay aware of what you're doing and *do a body scan — make yourself conscious of how it feels in your body*. When your mind wanders and you find yourself thinking about something else, bring your thoughts back to the present and simply stay aware of that.

"Do you know that you're breathing?"

Thich Nhat Hanh

HOW DO WE DEVELOP IN CONSCIOUSNESS?

We grow in consciousness in a very organic way, often in response to different conditions life presents to us. When that happens, we are required to consider how we'll respond. Will we choose to respond from an internal position of love? Or will we choose to react in fear?

As we become accomplished in solving problems presented to us in any given facet of consciousness, in any area of life, we take the skills and strengths we've developed along with us and dip into them whenever life presents conditions that require similar kinds of solutions.

Here is a *quick overview* of love and fear from within each facet of consciousness. We move from least expanded, in which we include just a small part of existence in our conception of who we are, to most expanded, in which we include all of existence in our definition of who we are in every area of life. Think of us as elastic bands of consciousness that increases in dimensionality and elasticity as we grow. Even though I'm describing the facets of consciousness here as if they are distinct, keep in mind that it is just for ease of communication. Inside of our real experience, they are more like relatively identifiable clumps of growth in life that bump into each other in both fluid and chaotic ways.

- From within the *Survive* facet of consciousness, the life conditions presented require us to solve very basic problems: the need for food, shelter, clothing, safety, and security. Love is experienced as the feeling of having enough of what I need. Fear is of the unknown and feelings of scarcity in any area of basic need. Once we've experienced not having enough of something, fear is always present in the background. It is most often experienced as an unnamed feeling of anxiety in the gut.

- The life conditions presented from within the *Belong* facet of consciousness require us to develop feelings of belonging to a group/family/religion/ culture. Love is experienced as feelings of belonging and loyalty. Fear is the possibility of being cast out or shunned by the group. Fear is present in the background of consciousness if we express disloyalty to the group, or if we observe another member of the group being cast out or shunned.

- The life conditions presented from within the *Individuate* facet of consciousness require us to do the work of individuating, most commonly from our parents, or the people who have raised us. Love is the experience of feeling the freedom and independence we achieve by doing this individuation work. Fear is the experience of feeling dependent on and perhaps controlled by our parents. Fear is almost always present in the background and it looks like bravado.

- The life conditions presented from within the *Comply* facet of consciousness require us to learn and adopt the rules of our family/culture/society/ religion/the road. The rules we adopt include our immediate culture's moral and ethical guidelines for behavior. Love is the experience of loyalty and adapting ourselves to fit the rules of acceptable behavior we've learned—we want to be good.

Fear is of the experience of losing acceptance and connection to our family/group/culture if we don't comply with the rules.

- The life conditions presented from within the *Re-individuate & Risk* facet of consciousness require us to think about the rules we adopted in the *Comply* facet, decide which of those rules no longer align with our core selves, and let go of them. In this facet, we become more self-referential. Love is the experience of feeling increasing empowerment, creativity, and willingness to take risks. Fear is of the possibility that I'll lose whatever is important to me because I'm stepping away from what is acceptable to my family/group/culture.

- Within the *Care & Empathy* facet of consciousness our core self expands in such a way that we come into a felt sense of relatedness to a larger community than we had previously identified as ours. We grow to care about all human beings as deeply as we care about those who belong to our family/group/etc. We grow to care about all biological creatures as deeply as we care about our own dogs or cats. And we grow to care about the living earth as deeply as we care about our own back yards. Love expands in to

19

the experience of care and empathy. Fear is the experience of feelings of being overwhelmed and inadequate.

- *And then, in some area of life, we move from Subsistence existence to Being. This move is from trying to be enough, have enough, care enough, work enough, to knowing that we are enough, that no matter how much we have, care, or work, it is enough. Being means that we have a relatively continuous felt sense of the connectivity of all that is and stay conscious in the present moment much more often than not.*

- When we're functioning primarily from **Integrate & Be Authentic**, we have thought deeply about our own beliefs and values and have integrated and live from them. Living authentically, being true to our Core Self is most important to us. Our values are derived from the realization and *felt sense* of the profound connectivity of all things—from the Wholeness of Life itself. We see Life and consciousness as an interconnected Whole and appreciate the strengths and skills we develop in every facet of consciousness. Love is the experience of connectivity and authenticity. We understand with the heart and work with purpose. We never take action from fear. As soon as we recognize fear, we acknowledge, thank, and transmute it.

- From within *Be Oneness* we experience ourselves and all of life as Oneness-of-Being, and the actions we take, the choices we make, even the thoughts we think, take this underlying connectivity of All-That-Is into consideration. Love is the felt sense experience of Oneness of Being, including the seen and the unseen world. Fear is felt as any disruption of this experience of Oneness. As soon as it is recognized, it is transmuted.

- Within the *Be Creation* facet of consciousness we experience everything-that-is as Sacred. Everything. There is no difference between the seen and unseen world. Love and Fear are simply parts of the whole. Neither one is personal. They are part of creation and are not identified as separate.

We might just be able to recognize when we are about to make a choice based on fear, stop ourselves and ask the question: "What would I do if I choose from love instead?" Use the handy-dandy brief description of Love and Fear at the beginning of each chapter on the different facets of consciousness to help you identify the fear if you're not sure what it is. A fear from one facet can often be addressed by taking an action based on love from the facet that follows it. Another way to think about it is to recognize that a choice from love will always enlarge our world. Love includes, expands, and allows. Fear excludes, shrinks, and tries to control.

Think of consciousness as being an aspect of the unseen world that is formless and fills all existent space. We are born inside of this potentiality of consciousness and our movement in it is fluid, interactive, sometimes playful, and sometimes difficult. There are no hard lines between facets of consciousness. Even as we live and develop ourselves primarily in one facet, we will likely have flashes of insight, experience of, and access to knowledge from other facets of consciousness.

An example that I think nearly everyone will relate to is the experience of Oneness-of-Being that can occur during a moment in which we are extremely present. Moments of extreme presence can happen as an internal response to being immersed in Epic Nature. Many of us are filled with this experience of wonder when we stand at the edge of an infinite view: the Grand Canyon, the shore of an ocean, in the mountains, or in a grove of redwoods. But extreme presence can come to us in many ways: lovers sharing a perfect moment just before the birth of their child, feeling like the end of an event can't come soon enough and then being absolutely engulfed in a wholehearted hug from Aunt Marge, or singing Dad's favorite hymns to him while he makes the journey out of his body.

The experience leaves us with a feeling of having been part of something Sacred, and it stays with us. It comes back to us periodically as one of our most memorable life experiences, and might even bring tears to our eyes. I remember having had this experience for the first time when I was about 26 years old. My husband won a trip from the Chamber of Commerce for five days and four nights on Maui. It was the first vacation I'd ever been on that required a flight. The wondrous moment happened one evening as I sat on the beach watching the sun set on the horizon over the Pacific Ocean. I had never actually been internally still and watched the sun set before, and the impact was profound. I had this very sacred experience of Oneness-of-Being as I sat there. It filled me with wonder. I carry that in my heart all these years later as one of the most profound and educational experiences of my life.

This Oneness-of-Being experience is continuous for human beings who live primarily from within the *Be Oneness* facet of consciousness.

The experience of extreme presence, noticing the sun setting on the horizon, and being perfectly, internally still in that moment, began to direct and shape my life. Within a few years, I was immersed in studying both psychology and philosophy at Purdue University, and in the study and practice of meditation with a local group led by Conrad and Ilene Satala. The combination of these three disciplines equates to the study of consciousness. I didn't know that at the time. I just knew that I was finally engaged in studying something that was profoundly helpful to me in the living of my everyday life.

Luckily, during the course of these last forty years, I've encountered others who have been deeply immersed in studying consciousness as well. They have each become lifelong friends and colleagues. Some of them belong to the Focus Group for this book. Their insight and intelligence helps to form this work.

One Action to Take Today to Explore Consciousness:

Whenever you become conscious of thinking about something that happened in the past, whether painful or pleasurable, say to yourself: "I thank you my past experience. I have learned from you." And bring yourself into the present moment.

Now, set the intention that any time your mind wanders into the past, you will become aware of it, repeat the feeling of gratitude for what you've learned, and move your mind back to the present moment.

THE SHAPE OF CONSCIOUSNESS

The shape of consciousness has historically been shown using designs that are both linear and hierarchical. Spirals, triangles, and squares containing other squares have all been used. Because our brain works in both a linear and hierarchical way, those designs have made sense to us. In fact, it's difficult to talk about consciousness in any other way. But we must try, because consciousness is neither linear nor hierarchical—it is much more fluid in the way that it interacts with us and in the way that we interact with it.

Members of the Focus Group for this book spent a lot of time working to come up with a model that would reflect our actual experience. In the first written iteration of this book, I used the wording "levels of consciousness" to describe the experience of growth. Everyone objected to that and someone suggested replacing "levels" with "stages", and we talked about it like that for a few weeks.

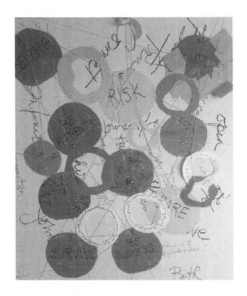

While we were in the "stage" phase, a couple of us came up with this design to portray how consciousness actually grows in us. Notice that every "stage" of consciousness is connected to every other "stage" in some way. Notice that *Comply* is surrounded by soft blue cushions of post it notes. That's because moving any area of life out of *Comply* can be extremely painful. This image from the Focus Group evokes the actual experience of how we grow in consciousness—it happens in the middle of the messiness of life itself, sometimes in just one area of life at a time, but most often in several areas of life at once. It is not orderly. And because life itself presents the conditions that demand growth from us, we can't control how it happens. What we can do is learn to understand the "stages" of consciousness

27

so we can recognize them as they occur, and perhaps be able to support ourselves in the middle of our own growth.

Once we worked with "stages" for a while, we felt the word inadequate to the task. It continued to imply neatness and orderliness that simply isn't true to the experience. We also became aware as we talked about each chapter that we couldn't help thinking of "stages" in which we include more of what exists in our perception of our self as being better than those in which we include a smaller portion of existence in our perception of who we are.

But the absolute truth is that we attain essential skills and strengths from each "stage" of consciousness. They are all necessary to our having the ability to fully express our humanity. Focus Group member Calvin suggested that we must come up with a model that expresses the random, sometimes chaotic messiness of how we grow, because the model we carry in our minds determines how we think and talk about it. He suggested we think of ourselves as an elastic band inside of a three dimensional expanse of consciousness. *Be Creation* is at the center, and the elastic band that is us stretches around pins representing all of the other "stages" of consciousness. When we grow in one area of life, the elastic band expands out in that direction.

As we continue to stretch in all the different directions, our consciousness grows in elasticity, depth, and strength.

And that is when the word, "stage" got replaced by the word, "facet."

I began to think about *facets of consciousness* intersecting with *life conditions* and *areas of life* as creating *clusters of learning experiences*. This eliminated both hierarchy and linearity in my mind and I remembered a photograph I took of my granddaughter many years ago. I held a multi-faceted egg shaped crystal up to the lens of my camera and this is the picture it produced.

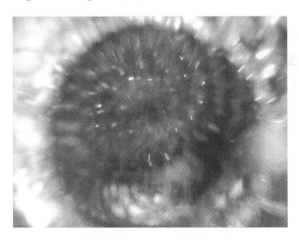

And, voila! We have a picture of our new model of consciousness. We are shown as extraordinary points of light expressing itself.

One Action to Take Today to Explore Consciousness:

Take a few minutes to remember a time when you were extremely present in a moment. Let yourself bathe in the memory, using as many of your senses as possible— especially ask to *feel it in the body*. If you haven't yet experienced this kind of awe, pursue it. Take a few minutes to just stop and watch the sun go down, ask someone you love for a wholehearted hug, or take a walk and place the palm of your hand on the bark of any tree, close your eyes, and get a felt sense of the aliveness of the tree. Bring all of your senses to the moment and notice the experience as completely as possible. Repeat every day.

Section Two

The Initial Six: *Survive, Belong, Individuate,*

Comply, Re-individuate & Risk, and Care & Empathy

The main feature that marks our thinking in these facets of consciousness is that we think there is only *one correct way* to see something, and that is the way in which *we* see it! This situation presents a problem for our relationship with others as individuals and for the social group/entire culture/whole world in which we live. *Disharmony erupts when we cannot understand that others may see it differently, and we feel we must force our perspective on to them.* I believe

31

that our most problematic human experiences are caused by this experience.

That circumstance is the main reason I am writing this book.

It is important that we understand that each one of us is living from within a facet of consciousness that has it's own perspective, and just like looking through a specific pair of glasses, *the facet determines how we see, experience, and interpret the world.* I am hoping that as you read about the different facets of consciousness, you will recognize others, from the inside of which, you have lived and experienced life. Then as you read about the facets of consciousness from which you have not yet lived, you will understand that you could see things from a different perspective than the one from which you now live.

I would imagine that if you live in the United States, you value living in a democracy. In order for us to maintain a healthy democracy, we must be able to dialogue civilly with each other, listen respectfully, openly, and strive to understand each other's point of view. When we're able to do that, we search for ways to compromise and create win/win solutions, which keeps our democracy healthy.

SURVIVE

Love and Fear

Love = Feelings of security and safety. I have enough of what I need.

Fear = Feelings of insecurity and that there won't be enough. Once we've experienced not having enough of something essential, fear is always present in the background, often experienced as an unnamed feeling in the gut.

Keep in mind that…

Consciousness is a cloud of potential awareness, part of the unseen world that permeates all of the space and material of existence. We grow in consciousness in response to different conditions life presents to us and must consider how we'll respond. Will we respond from an internal position of love, or will we choose to react in fear?

This facet of consciousness is focused on surviving. Our priority is in satisfying the basic human needs of food, water, warmth, sex, and safety. When we're functioning from within this facet of consciousness, we cannot think about anything other than these basic needs. If we feel physically threatened by a set of existing circumstances, all that we can think about is to do whatever is necessary to preserve our own lives.

It helps me to think of this facet of consciousness as describing all of the following:

- It is a facet of human development that we continuously go through, in every aspect of life, throughout our lives; and because of that, it is also
- A facet in which an aspect of ourselves can either participate or be stuck, while the dominant part of us lives from within a different facet of consciousness;
- And can be the dominant facet of consciousness expressed by a group, while individual members may be living from within another facet.

In the terrorist attack on the World Trade Center buildings that occurred on September 11, 2001, many people inside the buildings were immediately thrown into survival mode. They ran down the stairs with ferocity. They ran as fast as they could, the need to survive being the only one they could act on. We also have evidence that not everyone that day went into survival mode. We've heard about people who felt compelled to stop and stay with folks confined to wheelchairs who were physically unable to run down the stairs.

Is one action right, another wrong? For me, the answer has to be no. If there is only one option that presents itself, one internal call to follow, then it's neither right nor wrong. It simply is the only thing we can do.

For those who clicked into *Survive*, saving themselves was the only possible choice they could make. They couldn't have done anything but fly down those stairs as fast as they could go. Other options were simply unavailable to them. Whereas, those who stayed with folks who were unable to descend the stairs had clicked in to the *Care & Empathy* facet of consciousness, and because of that, the only possible choice they could make was to stay, to provide friendship and comfort. For these folks, the option to save themselves was unavailable.

We currently have circumstances in this world, in which human beings have been thrown into the life conditions that accompany this facet of consciousness—trying to figure out how to survive, how to get enough food, water, and shelter for themselves and their families. There are huge camps of refugees, fleeing for their lives from countries at war in various places on this planet.

In the United States of America, we have children who don't have some of these basic needs met. They go to school hungry because there isn't any food for them to eat at home. We also have a large population of homeless people. The causes are varied, of course, from veterans suffering from post-traumatic stress syndrome, folks who

are mentally ill, some people who are addicted to alcohol or another substance, and some who've lost a job and lack a support system of family or friends to give them an assist.

One example from my life of how a person or family who normally lives from a different facet of consciousness, can move into life conditions that call for problem solving skills and strengths learned in the *Survive* facet, happened when I was just a kid.

I was in the fifth grade when my dad had his first mental breakdown. That's what they called it at the time. When I read about post-traumatic stress syndrome, the condition many soldiers came home with from the Vietnam War, it sounded a lot like my dad. He served his country during World War II as a Marine in the South Pacific, and was the Radioman for his battalion. He told planes where to drop bombs. He witnessed men sacrifice their lives to save his. He was one of thirteen Marines left alive and physically unharmed in the battle of Sugarloaf Hill. The memory terrorized him.

To give you some idea of the horrifying conditions my dad, and other survivors, lived through, 1,656 Marines died and 7,429 were wounded during the twelve days that

it took to secure Sugar Loaf Hill. World War II ended shortly after that battle, but for my dad, and others like him, the internalized war never did end. Dad died when he was only sixty-six years old. A former Marine and fellow survivor of the battle for Sugar Loaf Hill came to Dad's funeral. He asked us why Dad's obituary didn't mention that he had been a member of the Sixth Marine Division. He felt that Dad should have been honored for his service. And he should have. In many ways, that experience defined his life, and had a profound effect on the way in which he lived with his wife and children.

My mom was completely deaf. Until she was in her forties, there was no hearing aid strong enough to help her hear. Because of that, Dad talked to us kids. Many nights at the dinner table, beginning when I was in second grade, my dad talked about his experience during World War II. It was obvious, even to a six year old, that my dad was tormented by his experience. He also displayed episodes of extreme violence toward Mom and to many of us kids.

After one of those extremely violent episodes, Dad was admitted to the VA Hospital for treatment. He was given a diagnosis and an antipsychotic prescription that eventually helped him to live more of a normal life.

When Dad entered the hospital, Mom went to talk to the company Dad worked for to find out how to go about getting his disability pay. There were six of us kids at home at that time, and Mom and Dad lived from paycheck to paycheck. She was told it would be two weeks before a check would be available. I remember Mom being shocked. For the first time in her life, she was faced with the task of having to put food on the table, with no money in reserve and no time to waste. She scrambled!

Mom went to get food stamps and came home furious! She hated having to ask for a handout! She also went to a food bank and got huge containers of Velveeta cheese and peanut butter. And she hated doing that too! She went to the day-old bread store and bought outdated loaves of bread for ten cents a loaf. She sold our upright piano for $50, and that helped some. After my older sister and I got home from school, she left us to babysit while she went door to door in the neighborhood selling a very good brand of clothing called Minnesota Woolens.

Mom had been raised in a blue-collar working class family. Her parents were very proud of the fact that they made it through the depression without having to ask for help. When Mom's dad was laid off, he knocked on the doors of the largest homes in town and found work painting the exteriors of houses. Their pride at not having had to ask

for a handout, and the disdain they voiced about those who did, shaped Mom's values and made it very hard for her to ask for and accept help.

With Dad in the hospital, Mom clicked into this *Survive* facet of consciousness. She was determined to do whatever she had to do to keep herself and us fed and sheltered. A new resolve was born in her too.

When Mom graduated from high school, she had been offered a full scholarship to Saint Francis College, but because of her inability to hear, her mom and dad encouraged her to marry my dad instead. They wanted her to be taken care of because of her hearing impairment. During this time, when she had to scramble for food and money to take care of herself and us, her lack of education and ability to hear, meant that any job she might have been interested in doing was unavailable to her.

She became determined to get an education so that she would never be in a situation again in which she couldn't support herself or her kids if anything happened to my dad.

When Mom was 40, she applied to college at Indiana University. She earned a bachelor's degree in history and then went on to earn a master's degree in library science. She also got her dream job, which was to work as a librarian.

This piece of my own life story is a perfect example of someone who was living predominantly within another facet of consciousness, but because of new life conditions, was thrown into *Survive*.

What it looks like to be artificially stuck in *Survive*:

Remember, this facet of consciousness has to do with finding food, water, warmth, sex, and safety. Given the rising rates of obesity and diabetes in the United States, I think it's safe to say that many of us are artificially stuck in *Survive* regarding food.

There are good reasons for it, of course. All we have to do is understand that sugar is addictive, then read ingredients on everything we buy that is a manufactured food. What we'll find is that sugar in one form or another is included in almost everything we eat. In the body, these foods break down very quickly, leaving us hungry and searching for more food. We're constantly on the hunt for something else to eat.

A couple of years ago, I was in this quandary myself. The doctor informed me that I was pre-diabetic. I could turn it around, he said, but in order to do so, I could not eat sugar in any form. That included all of the sugars I thought were supposed to be good as well—sugars like honey, maple syrup, agave syrup, and etc. The doc also told me to stay away from all grains. All grains! Even the organic, whole grains! Unfortunately, at that time, my favorite breakfast had been toast made from a whole-grain, organic, molasses bread that I'd been buying at the local farmer's market. Other foods I was not allowed to eat were white potatoes, pasta, or rice—neither white nor brown. I was only allowed to eat whole foods—more vegetables than anything else, and fruits that are low-glycemic, meaning they don't break down quickly in the body.

I was cranky and crabby for about a week when I stopped eating this stuff.

The benefit of eliminating these foods is that I feel full longer and am not hunting for something to eat all the time. The artificial condition of being stuck in *Survive* was eliminated.

One Action to Take Today to Explore Consciousness:

Take a moment to think about whether you feel safe and secure. Do a head to toe body scan and ask yourself what safety feels like in your body? Do you fear not having enough of any basic human need—food, water, shelter, warmth, or safety? Just become aware. Now take a moment to feel thankful for basic needs that are met in this moment, and now in this moment. Repeat gratitude daily.

BELONG

Love and Fear

Love = feelings of belonging and loyalty to the group.

Fear = the possibility of being cast out or shunned by the group. Fear is present in the background of consciousness if we have either expressed disloyalty to the group, or observed another member of the group being cast out.

Keep in mind that...

Consciousness is a cloud of potential awareness, part of the unseen world that permeates all of the space and material of existence. We grow in consciousness in response to different conditions life presents to us and must consider how we'll respond. Will we respond from an internal position of love, or will we choose to react in fear?

In this facet of consciousness, we are concerned with the well being of *our* family, *our* group, *our* country, *our* religion, *because they are ours.* The family/clan/gang/club/team/political party contains the people who matter. Everyone else is an outsider, (maybe even) a non-person, and a potential threat. This inward focus of group members serves to isolate us. The deeper the entrenchment is, the larger the separation from outsiders, human beings who don't belong to the group. This makes different points of view, new ideas, ways of thinking, and discoveries unavailable to us. Groups living in this facet of consciousness create very powerful feelings of belonging among members, and use symbols and rituals to help establish that. In this facet of consciousness, our life and loyalty belongs to the group.

Sacred words and symbols can invoke this meme in us—they give us a feeling of pride and belonging. When we sing the national anthem in a stadium filled with the voices of people singing, feelings of belonging can be so great that tears spring to our eyes. In church, when everyone is singing the familiar hymn, "Amazing Grace," we might experience that deep sense of belonging. And just imagine the explosion of pride and feelings of belonging for Cub fans during the 7th inning at Wrigley Field, when fans participated in the ritual of singing "Take Me Out to the Ballgame" the night the Cubs won the Series in 2016. I wasn't there, but I know the win Cubs fans witnessed caused tears to stream down the faces of all who were present.

It helps me to think of this facet of consciousness as describing all of the following:

- It is a facet of human development, beginning in childhood that we continuously go through, in every aspect of life, throughout our lives, and because of that, it is also
- A facet in which an aspect of ourselves can either participate or be stuck, while the dominant part of us lives from within a different facet of consciousness;

- And can be the dominant facet of consciousness expressed by a group, while individual members may be functioning within another facet.
- And can be used by leaders to call us to express our highest nature in committing acts of care or kindness, or be used to manipulate us into doing unthinkable harm.

Childhood feelings of belonging to my family of origin meant that we eight siblings defended each other fiercely in any situation. It didn't matter who was right or wrong, we defended our own. When one of my little brothers had his bag of candy stolen while we were trick-or-treating on Halloween night, his older siblings ran after the thief. My older sister caught the little bugger and returned our brother's bag of candy to him. This kind of loyalty also meant that we never disclosed to anyone the violent behavior that erupted from my dad, as he succumbed to a mental breakdown, no matter how severe his behavior was.

A good example of this kind of fierce loyalty to one's own group/tribe/family can be seen in the individual Clans of the Scottish Highlanders. A few years ago, I attended the Highland Games in Scotland and witnessed some of this fierce loyalty. Before the Queen arrived, the announcer requested emphatically over the loud speaker that attendees stand when the Queen entered her private viewing box, and that they sing "God Save the Queen" with robust enthusiasm. Not everyone stood when Queen Elizabeth entered, and the song was sung by most, if somewhat tepidly. I was told that it is the Queen's favorite yearly event, so I suppose she's used to that cool reception. The Scottish People are loyal to their own, and it looks like they still resent having an English Monarchy. After she arrived, a thousand or more Clansmen marched into the arena, all dressed and grouped in their individual Clan tartans. Most Clan members were carrying bagpipes, and playing a tune that was both mournful and voluminous—think of it--nearly a thousand bagpipes, playing the same tune! There was, however, one Clan from the Scottish Highlands, Clan MacDonald, in which individual members all carried twelve-foot-long spears and looked extraordinarily fierce as they marched past the Queen's private viewing box!

When we are primarily expressing life from within another facet of consciousness, most of us will dip into the healthy aspects of *Belong* to strengthen feelings of belonging and connection with others. Using what we learned in this facet of consciousness, we create family rituals that endure. Examples from my family of origin are that we hold hands and say what we're thankful for before Thanksgiving dinner. We also gather together at the family cottage for the July 4th weekend to play together—that's between 30 and 50 people, all cooking, swimming and playing games with each other. For many years, on Memorial Day weekend, we met at one of my sister's homes in Southern Indiana for an annual family bike race that was plotted out carefully by my brother-in-law. We had t-shirts made to commemorate the race, designed by artistically inclined family members—one for each year. I loved the tradition and still have all of my t-shirts. When I wear one of them, it evokes feelings of belonging and love for my family.

We can find tons of healthy examples of this *Belong* facet of consciousness being expressed by groups of people in our culture. On any given Sunday, we will find people, who very likely live from within a more expanded facet of consciousness, participating in the Sunday morning ritual at church. On Sunday afternoons, we can find huge numbers of people watching favorite teams play in stadiums or on television. We are supplicants together and we are fans together. One of my good friends has the ritual of watching the Packers games together as a family (emphasis on their being together). When one family member wasn't going to arrive home from a trip until the game had already been played, the family recorded the game and all swore not to watch any part of it until their daughter arrived home that evening. Then they sat down together to cheer their team on and dispute the Ref's calls!

Watching the Olympic games invokes feelings of pride

and belonging. Some of us may even feel a sense of pride and belonging to humanity itself—an experience that weaves us together into one community, striving for physical and mental excellence. Some of those Olympic events create such enormous feelings of belonging that they never leave us. One such event for me was the 800-meter race at the 1972 Summer Olympics when I watched Dave Wottle, who was running in last place, overtake each competitor, one after another to win the gold medal. It was one of the most exciting events I've ever watched. I found it on YouTube so I could watch it again. I cried the first time I watched that race and when I saw it again, it still made me cry.

When leaders call us to express our highest nature in committing acts of care, kindness, or service, this is one of the facets of consciousness they are invoking. On January 20, 1961, in his Inaugural Address, John F. Kennedy said, "…my fellow Americans: ask not what your country can do for you—ask what you can do for your country." That is the part of his Address that I have always remembered, even though I was just a little kid at the time. It was meaningful to me and evoked feelings of pride and belonging. I didn't remember the sentence that followed, but I think it's worth noting here. President Kennedy also said, "My fellow citizens of the world: ask not what America will do for you, but what together we can do for the freedom of man." On March 1, 1961, President John F.

Kennedy issued an Executive Order to establish the Peace Corps as a new agency within the Department of State. Young people from all over the United States followed a call to serve their country in the Peace Corps, and young people continue to do so today.

When leaders reach into and use the unhealthy aspects of this *Belong* facet of consciousness in us, it can dissolve basic human decency. History provides a record of human beings who have been manipulated into committing unthinkable harm. This is the dynamic that has led to ethnic cleansing and racial violence all over the world, and it continues to do so today. It is the dynamic Hitler used when he set about creating a "pure race" of German people by killing Jewish people and others. At times in United States history, leaders have ennobled the racist KKK and White Supremacy groups. Japanese Kamikaze pilots represented this facet of consciousness during WWII, as did the terrorists who flew planes into the World Trade Center buildings on 9/11/2001.

One Action to Take Today to Explore Consciousness:

Think about your feelings of belonging and loyalty and
what groups these feelings happen within. Do you alter
yourself in any way to match the group's expectations of
you? Are you loyal first to yourself and is that reflected in
your expression of who you are while you're with them?
What does it feel like in the body to belong to the group?
What does it feel like in the body to belong to yourself?
Notice if there is a difference.

INDIVIDUATE

Love and Fear

Love = the feeling of freedom and independence
that comes with the action of individuating from
our parents/family/ group.

Fear = the feeling of being dependent on, and the
inability to be independent from our
parents/family/group. This fear is nearly always in
the background from within this facet, and looks
like bravado.

> ## Keep in mind that…
>
> Consciousness is a cloud of potential awareness, part of the unseen world that permeates all of the space and material of existence. We grow in consciousness in response to different conditions life presents to us and must consider how we'll respond. Will we respond from an internal position of love, or will we choose to react in fear?

In this *Individuate* facet of consciousness, we are driven to separate ourselves from our parents and proclaim to ourselves and to our world that we are independent people. The ego emerges in our psyche and begins this individuation process, in small bursts at first. Think about a three-year-old child, proclaiming loudly: "I do it myself!" Even though the process of individuation occurs in every area of life throughout our lives, we often work especially hard at this when we're teenagers.

During our teenage years, this work is fraught with potential danger because our prefrontal cortex isn't fully developed,[1] and that means we function primarily from

the feeling part of the brain until we're about twenty-five. The process of reasoning and the understanding that we could die is a function of the prefrontal cortex. We don't realize that our actions could have life-threatening consequences for ourselves and for others. Is it any wonder that many of us look back at ourselves as teenagers with amazement that we actually lived through those years?

We can think of this facet of consciousness as describing all of the following:

- It is a facet of human development that we continuously go through, in every aspect of life, throughout our lives; and because of that, it is also
- A facet in which an aspect of ourselves can either participate or be stuck, while the dominant part of us lives from within a different facet of consciousness;
- And can be the dominant facet of consciousness expressed by a group, while individual members may be functioning from within another.

From within *Individuate*, our thinking is egocentric. We want what we want and we want it now! We act on

---

[1] There is a multitude of research available in neuroscience to support this claim. If you would like to learn more about this, a cursory web search on prefrontal cortex development will give you as much information as you would like.

impulse rather than forethought, and are unable to conjure up what the consequences of our actions may be. Because we're unable to imagine what might happen as a result of our actions, punishment and threats don't work to control or teach us. Any difficulties or failures we encounter are always someone else's fault. We don't have feelings of guilt or remorse because we don't accept blame or responsibility for anything that goes wrong.

Here are some examples of the *Individuate* facet of consciousness.

I came home from work one day when my son was thirteen years old and found him sitting outside on the front porch swing. His boom box was blaring Heavy Metal music as loud as the setting would go. He was having his kind of fun, with no regard for anyone else at all. I'm sure the neighbors were glad when I returned home and turned the music down. I remember doing the same thing when I was that age. I just used different equipment and different music—a record player and a vinyl 45 of "The Duke of Earl" blasted to the max when I was babysitting for my nieces.

Many of us experience this facet of consciousness in more subtle ways. I remember beginning the process of

individuating at school first. I rebelled against the interminable boredom of repetitive worksheets on which we were supposed to practice math concepts. I would write any number that came into my head as an answer, turn the worksheet in to the teacher in minutes, and move on to the more interesting business of doing art. I already knew how to add, subtract, multiply, and divide, and saw no reason to actually practice the skill by doing the problems. It was a small rebellious act, but it infuriated and frustrated my poor teachers. I always passed to the next grade, but no one was ever happy with the work I did. I also rebelled on the coloring worksheets. I never followed the directions; never stayed inside the lines—they were boring too. Instead, I used the brightest colors in the crayon box, and made my own design. No one was ever happy with that either.

At home, I rebelled by lying to my parents. I felt that I couldn't tell the whole truth and be able to do what I wanted to do. Once I told Mom and Dad that a friend's parent would bring us home from the Roller Dome at the end of the evening, when in truth, I was going by myself and no one was lined up to bring me home. I had an extra dollar, above what I needed for entrance and skate rental, so my plan was to call a taxi and have the taxi take me as close to home as a dollar would go. I planned to walk the rest of the way.

Mom dropped me off at the Roller Dome, (because lie number two was that my friend was going to meet me there). I loved to roller skate! And I loved to dance! Most of my lying rebellion was done to enable me to do one or the other. At the end of that particular lying-event-evening, I called a taxi. When I got in the cab, I told the taxi driver that I had one dollar, told him where I lived, and asked him to take me as close to the address as he could, and I would walk the rest of the way home. The Roller Dome was about four miles from my house and it was around midnight. (Can't you hear him swearing under his breath?) I was just a skinny little eleven-year-old, who had never taken a taxi before and had no idea how it worked. He took me to within four blocks of my house, and I walked the rest of the way home. I am grateful for his generosity to this day. In case you're wondering, I did get caught once in a while, and then would be grounded for weeks, sometimes months! I definitely deserved it.

My daughter's individuation process was very subtle. When she was growing up, we lived in northern Indiana, and the winters there can be very cold. When she left the house to walk to school, I would make sure that she was all bundled up. The minute after she walked out the door, she would unzip, unbutton, remove her hat and mittens and stuff them into coat pockets, and sometimes remove

her coat entirely. She would claim that she was too hot, but I think there was rebellion in that gesture. It's the only example that I could think of in which she completely rejected what I wanted her to do.

My daughter believes that her individuation process happened most profoundly when she chose to study marine biology after high school. It meant that we had to move her from the Midwest to one of the only available programs, thousands of miles away on the coast of California. Away from her parents, she created life in the way that she wanted to live it and thrived.

I've talked to friends about this individuation process and asked them to share their stories with me. One friend told me that when she was growing up, she never, ever rebelled against the wishes of her parents or teachers. She is the oldest child in the family and was continuously told by her parents that she must set a good example for her younger siblings. My friend said she never rebelled in school either. Her desire was to be perfect—for her parents, her teachers, and herself. The domestication process[2] was so thorough and intense for her that she

---

[2] To learn more about the "domestication process" that we all undergo in varying degrees when we're children, read *The Mastery of Love*, by Don Miguel Ruiz. "Domestication" is also a concept employed by Paolo Freire in *Pedagogy of the*

remained identified with the family group, moving from her parent's house to her husband's house without ever having rebelled against or about anything. That didn't happen until she was forty years old. She undomesticated herself, individuated, divorced, and began living life in the way that was satisfying and fulfilling to her.

The work of individuating can happen at different ages. It isn't a process that is locked in to the hormone pounding teenage years.

We can recognize an *aspect of ourselves that might be stuck* in this facet of consciousness, by examining where we want *instant gratification*. The behavior might be expressed in shopping or gambling, even though the credit card balances are already high. We might buy that new diet pill that promises huge weight loss in short time periods.

Another cue we can use to recognize whether *we might be stuck* in *Individuate* is when we look to *blame someone else* for something that goes wrong. We can't correct a problem if we don't take responsibility for our part in having created it.

Oppressed, a term he uses to describe a systematic societal process of teaching oppressed people to internalize their inferiority in order to maintain social control in a hierarchy.

One Action to Take Today to Explore Consciousness:

Are there any times that you want instant gratification and act on that? Think about one of those times and decide to make a conscious choice to put planning into the circumstance and extend gratification to a later date. Think about any experience in which you've placed blame on someone else. Give power back to yourself by identifying your part in what happened. Notice what your body feels like when you blame. Notice what your body feels like when you take responsibility for your part.

COMPLY

Love and Fear

Love = The feeling of loyalty to the
family/group/culture—we want to learn its rules, and
take them on as ours, because we want to feel
connected in a way that goes beyond the feeling of
belonging.

Fear = If I don't comply with the rules, I will disappoint
them (my family, group, culture), won't be accepted by
them anymore and will lose my connection to the
group.

Keep in mind that…

Consciousness is a cloud of potential awareness,
part of the unseen world that permeates all of the
space and material of existence. We grow in
consciousness in response to different conditions
life presents to us and must consider how we'll
respond. Will we respond from an internal
position of love, or will we choose to react in fear?

This facet of consciousness describes the way in which we
learn and adopt the rules of our family/group/culture and
we learn the consequences we'll suffer for breaking them.
We begin to believe in a system that gives us an experience
of order into which we will anchor our moral, ethical and
civil behavior. The rules and consequences contain the
culture's ideas about right and wrong and we begin to
strive to implement them in our lives. We very likely take
on the belief that the ideas and values that our group holds
are the only right ones, the ones that should be held by
everyone.

As we enter into and live from this facet of consciousness
in any area of life, the need for certainty and
dependability, order and control is a priority. We want to
know our own proper social role, caste, grade, race, class,

seniority level, military rank, etc., and we want to know where everyone else fits into that schema too. During childhood we begin to take notice of how others are valued and how we are valued. Often unconsciously we begin to take on those messages about our relative worth, and then live and create our lives as if the messages are true.

Remember that this facet of consciousness describes all of the following:

- It is a facet of human development that we continuously go through, in every aspect of life, throughout our lives; and because of that, it also is
- A facet in which an aspect of ourselves can either participate or be stuck, while the dominant part of us lives from within a different facet of consciousness;
- And can be the dominant facet expressed by a group, while individual members may be functioning from within another facet.

It is helpful to recognize that our thinking from within this facet can be very rigid and dogmatic. We can be very judgmental, lack understanding, and be intolerant of the perspective expressed by others. We see things as being absolutely right or absolutely wrong; we find fault and we assign blame. We likely use guilt, shame and fear of punishment to control our own behavior and the behavior of others. We may even invoke the sacred name of God to punish the offenders (or think to ourselves that Karma will get them). We believe our version of truth will be shown to be *the* one and only *Truth*.

From within this facet of consciousness, Love equals the feeling of connection and belonging we gain by investing our loyalty in the culture first. We want to learn its rules, and try to make life into an acceptable version of them. Fear is in the knowledge that if we don't comply with the cultural rules, we will no longer be accepted by the family/group/culture and lose our felt sense of connection and belonging. Our fear may be great enough that it causes us to live perfectly what we've been taught to feel is our proper social role.

Once we become conscious of an internal constriction or tension while trying to live a proper version of a culturally acceptable role, we are faced with a choice. This is tough because *the very rules we internalize within this facet of consciousness create the embedded structures that can begin to feel limiting to us.* As we become conscious of an internalized structure that feels limiting and challenge its validity in our lives, we grow as conscious human beings, and become more aligned with our own core self. Often we take this risk in one area of life at a time.

Because we anchor our moral, ethical and civil behavior in the cultural rules and mores we develop within this facet, and because we feel so completely loyal to the family/group/ culture, taking a risk in any area of life can be as difficult as a divorce. But when we become aware of a rule that no longer aligns with our core self, at some point, we must find a way to move our loyalty *from culture to self* in that area. That inner move to break from societal rules and invest instead in our core self is a signal that we have effectively moved into a more expanded facet of consciousness in this area of life. That's how it normally happens—with one piece of life at a time, we divorce ourselves from an idea of rightness the culture in which we are immersed holds, and move into an idea of rightness that we hold for ourselves.

We begin this process of staying true to ourselves in a thousand ways, both large and small.

Here are some examples of cultural rules we learn in this facet of consciousness that stay with us and serve us well through the course of our lives.

In the United States, we take driver's education classes to

learn the rules of the road. We have to demonstrate our knowledge of those rules in both a written and a driving test before we're allowed the privilege of a driver's license. My dad taught me how to drive. Once I sped up to get through a yellow light before it turned red. Dad said, "Reggie, yellow lights mean slow down and prepare to stop. They don't mean speed up and hurry to get through the intersection!" You can imagine how often I've wished other drivers had learned how to drive from my dad! In fact, it's become essential to check the rear view mirror when coming up to a yellow light to make sure the person behind me isn't stepping on the gas!

Another example is the process of learning how to cook. We are likely taught how to follow a recipe, and the importance of measuring correctly for the success of the dish. As we acquire more experience and skill in following a recipe, we might simply continue making the dish in exactly that way throughout our lives. But at some point, we might begin to feel constricted by the recipe and decide to change it up by imagining the dish with other ingredients or spices. If the dish is Mom's traditional recipe for three-bean salad, a dish that has been made exactly the same way for every family gathering throughout history, making it an unwritten family rule, and you decide to eliminate the sugar and add cumin, you will get some (hopefully) good-natured flack. (Trust me on that.)

The same thing can happen with living a culturally acceptable version of a "proper" woman or man, or in the process of belonging to or leaving a church, or in leaving the career we initially pursue, or…(you get the idea).

We can recognize a*n aspect of ourselves that might be stuck* in this facet of consciousness, by examining where we feel constricted, and not aligned with our core self in an aspect of our lives.

One Action to Take Today to Explore Consciousness:

Think about any felt sense of discomfort you experience because you are following an internalized rule that no longer suits you. Notice what that discomfort feels like in the body. What one thing could you bravely do today to live more authentically aligned with your own core self?

RE-INDIVIDUATE & RISK

Love and Fear

Love = Feelings of empowerment, creativity, and the willingness to risk.

Fear = I might lose whatever it is that's important to me because I'm stepping away from what is acceptable to my family/group/culture.

> ## Keep in mind that...
>
> Consciousness is a cloud of potential
> awareness, part of the unseen world that
> permeates all of the space and material of
> existence. We grow in consciousness in
> response to different conditions life presents
> to us and must consider how we'll respond.
> Will we respond from an internal position
> of love, or will we choose to react in fear?

If we move into this *Re-individuate & Risk* facet of
consciousness in any area of life, it means that living by a
culturally accepted rule now feels so constricting that we
must stop living by it. We feel discomfort because the rule
doesn't align with our core self and because of that, feels
irrelevant and possibly even obstructive to our lives. This
can happen in any area of life. As I said in the last chapter,
moving out of a role that is socially acceptable to align
with inner truth from our core self can feel as painful as a
divorce. After we've taken this step often enough, the fear
we feel in the *Comply* facet of consciousness is no longer
able to control us. We begin to live more areas of life in
alignment with our core self.

Remember that this facet of consciousness describes all of the following:

- It is a facet of human development that we continuously go through, in every aspect of life, throughout our lives; and because of that, it also is
- A facet in which an aspect of ourselves can either participate or be stuck, while the dominant part of us lives from within a different facet of consciousness;
- And can be the dominant facet of consciousness expressed by a group, while individual members may be primarily functioning from within another facet.

Think of this move into the *Re-individuate & Risk* facet of consciousness as an uptick in independent, critical, and creative thinking. What does it look like in life when we stop following a rule or stop trying to live a version of ourselves that no longer fits? Have you ever stood up to a friend when he or she has said something racist, and risked losing that friend? Have you stopped someone who is objectifying or catcalling a woman or girl, and risked being maligned yourself? Have you come out to your family and friends as gay, lesbian, or transgender, and risked losing them? Have you ever left a church because it no longer supported your spiritual growth, and risked losing family and friends who still belong to that church? Have you ever had to stand up to a bully at work and risked losing your job? Have you decided to eat vegetarian food even though you're immersed in a family culture that is all about meat, and risked being ridiculed? These are all examples of personal *Re-individuation & Risk*. It takes courage to be true to ourselves when who we have become goes against the grain of the family/group/culture in which we are immersed.

One of the ways this shift from *Comply* into *Re-individuate & Risk* occurred in my personal life is that I've stopped trying to create the structure of an idealized marriage. We begin learning about it in the fairy tales of early childhood and that story had a very strong hold on me. I have been married and divorced four times. In our society, that is viewed as failure on a fairly grand scale.

I used to feel that way about myself too. I thought something was lacking in me—"if I were a better person, maybe one of those marriages would have lasted." Now I view it both as an education and a personal journey, one that has been filled with the risk of losing family and friends with each divorce. My family of origin was Catholic, a religion in which divorce is forbidden. But even without that background, our culture views 50th wedding anniversaries as a huge cause for celebration, and more than one divorce as cause for ridicule and embarrassment.

I want to tell you about this part of my life because we can have the idea that moving from one facet of consciousness into another is clean and happens all at once. It can be that way. But most of the time, it's messy and the process is slow and difficult.

I left the last marriage when the risk of staying became much greater than the risk of leaving, and when leaving became the only answer to the question: "What would Love do if the answer includes me?"

The fairy tale story of love was yet to be rewritten in me. During my last marriage, I painted two oil paintings of my husband and myself, setting the intention with every brushstroke that the love we shared would be large enough to sustain us. When I left him, I brought the paintings with me, along with a mixed media artwork that friends Cheryl and Ellen had created for my fourth husband and I for our wedding. When I settled into my apartment and unpacked the paintings, they simply made me feel sad.

I thought about burning them—making it a ceremony by doing it with friends. When I told my friend Ellen what I was thinking about doing, she suggested that it might be more useful to create something new with it instead of just letting the artwork go up in smoke. I cut the two portraits into strips and my friend Cheryl helped me weave one into the other.

"Reweaving the Patriarchal Story of Love."[3]

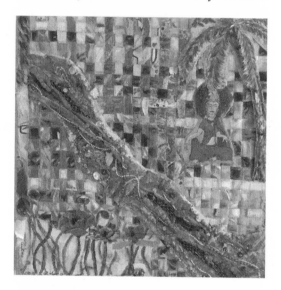

30"x30" Mixed Media

Contributing Artists: Ellen Sauer, Cheryl Spieth Gardner, and Regina Leffers

---

[3] If you would like to see this in color, go to reginaleffers.com.

I stitched the weaving together, and stitched the little portrait of Kwan Yin[4] onto the weaving. Then I appliqued pieces of Cheryl and Ellen's mixed media artwork onto the weaving. That's Ellen's river and palm tree and Cheryl's poppies and little handmade ceramic fish, shells, and stars that are sprinkled throughout. Now this piece, "Reweaving the Patriarchal Story of Love," hangs in my living room, and when I look at it, instead of sadness, I feel joy. I actually feel joy. The fairy tale story of love has been rewoven inside of me, and I am released from its hold.

I have always felt differently at my core with my friends than I have with a partner. I didn't always know that—it lived beneath the surface of my own consciousness. With a partner, I felt ultimately unlovable, unworthy, and unwanted. Because of that, I felt the need to continually prove to my partner that I deserved to be loved, wanted, and treated as worthy. With my friends, I have always felt the opposite. I know that I am loved and accepted *exactly* as I am.

My partners treated me as I treated myself within the partnership. My friends treat me as I treat myself within the friendship.

---

[4] Kwan Yin is the Buddhist Bodhisattva of Compassion.

Recognizing that difference and the mirrored quality—from/in my brain, to/in my world—allowed me to get to the underlying subconscious material and unpack it.

My friend John Beams, who is also a member of this book's Focus Group, brought the following quote from Thomas Keating to me. I love it because it does a good job of explaining why one area of life may be stuck within one facet of consciousness, while we live predominantly within another facet. Father Keating says:

> "We can have a mystical experience at any stage of development. But if we have…no practice to heal our early emotional wounds, that energy is not digested. If you have high graces and mystical unions, but other lines of development are incomplete, then the shadow will appear, even as you move forward spiritually."[5]

Translated into the language of consciousness,

_____

[5] From an interview: www.conniezweig.com. "A Spiritual Life Review with Father Thomas Keating." Dr. Connie Zweig. The Reinvention of Age. March 27, 2018.

Keating is saying that even as we explore multiple facets of consciousness, and live predominantly within a more expanded facet, unhealed material in any area of life can keep us stuck within a less expanded facet.

When we leave a marriage or church, or do anything to align with our own truth, our own core self, but that goes against the grain of our dominant family/group/culture, we can take those actions from love or from fear. If we take the action from fear, we will likely feel victimized and find ourselves bashing the person/church/etc. If on the other hand, we take the action from love, we will find ourselves looking for lessons learned and being grateful for the experience. It is always possible to stop bashing and look for lessons learned.

Gratitude is a transformative tool.

One Action to Take Today to Explore Consciousness:

Think about what *love* is in *Re-individuate & Risk*—feelings of empowerment, creativity, and the willingness to risk. Ask yourself to feel what that *love* feels like *in the body*. Now think about what *fear* is in *Re-individuate & Risk*—I might lose whatever it is that's important to me because I'm stepping away from what is acceptable to my family/group/culture. What does that *fear* feel like *in the body*? Notice any areas of life where these thoughts or feelings are present. Ask yourself to inhale the feeling, and exhale peace into that feeling. Repeat several times. Repeat whenever you feel fear of any kind.

CARE & EMPATHY

Love and Fear

Love expands to take the form of care and empathy.

Fear takes the form of feeling overwhelmed and inadequate.

Keep in mind that...

Consciousness is a cloud of potential awareness, part of the unseen world that permeates all of the space and material of existence. We grow in consciousness in response to different conditions life presents to us and must consider how we'll respond. Will we respond from an internal position of love, or will we choose to react in fear?

Moving into the *Care & Empathy* facet of consciousness means that our core self expands in such a way that we experience a felt sense of relatedness to a larger community than we had previously identified as ours. We grow to *care about (more of) the human race* as deeply as we care about those who belong to our family/group/religion, and so on. We grow to *care about (more of) the earth's biological creatures* as deeply as we care about our own dogs or cats. And we grow to *care about (more of) the living earth* as deeply as we care about our own back yards.

Living life from within *Care & Empathy*, we want deeper and more satisfying relationships. We explore our inner selves, and develop caring inter-relationships with our community. We begin to notice some of the injustices inherent in our society and decide to act—to do our part to make a social change. If we're billionaires like Bill and Melinda Gates, we might start a foundation and decide to eradicate a specific problem in third-world countries. If we're like most of us, we might change the course of our working life, or begin volunteering at a local food kitchen.

Remember that *Care & Empathy* describes all of the following:

- It is a facet of human development that we continuously go through, in every aspect of life, throughout our lives; and because of that, it also is
- A facet in which an aspect of ourselves can either participate or be stuck, while the dominant part of us lives from within a different facet of consciousness;
- And can be the dominant facet of consciousness expressed by a group, while individual members may be functioning within a different facet.

When we're living in *Care & Empathy*, we get excited and energized by working on projects together with others. Everyone is expected to speak up and contribute both ideas and feelings. Decisions take longer because our goal is to reach consensus, but we're willing to spend the time because we believe each voice has inherent worth. As long as members are interested enough to be informed and have the ability to understand the issues, this method works.

We actively work to build community and unity. We value peace, love and caring for others. We recognize that we are interdependent creatures, biologically, emotionally, and spiritually. This leads us to introspection—we want to understand ourselves as well as those with whom we're connected.

Social causes, volunteer health care agencies, soup kitchens, and affirmative action programs all arise within *Care & Empathy*. When enough people in a society value every individual, we create social movements and volunteer organizations that express that value. We want to blur the lines between the categories that can separate us, like gender and race.

An example of this kind of "blurring the lines" is illustrated by a meme that has been expressed for years, whether presented on television, billboards, or social media. The first picture shows a brown egg sitting beside a white egg on the kitchen counter. In the next picture, both eggs are shown, looking identical in a frying pan.

The idea is to show that even though we may look different on the outside, we're all one race—the human race—and we are all the same inside. The problem with this perspective is that when we collapse cultures, colors, and genders into one category, the human race, we gloss over the systems that privilege one flavor of human being over the other, allowing systemic "isms" to continue unchallenged.

We feel the collective guilt for all the wrongs human beings have committed toward groups of people who represent cultures and nationalities different from our own. One example is the historical lie we learn in grade school—that Columbus discovered America in 1492. In truth, he navigated to a body of land, and claimed that land for Spain. What we've come to call the United States of America was already populated. There is a movement in the United States, on which some states have already acted, to change "Columbus Day" to "Indigenous American Day".

Experiencing the feeling of empathy, the ability to put yourself in someone else's shoes and feel what they feel, can happen at any age. It happened for me when I was about seven or eight years old. I grew up in a house that was about two blocks from a railroad track. This was in the early 1950's and homeless men still rode the rails.

They would hop on an open railcar and find a place to sleep. Then they'd hop off when they needed to find something to eat. We called them "hobos" back then. Occasionally, we would see them walking through the alley during the summer.

One time my dad saw a hobo looking through our garbage can. Dad went outside and the man took off running. My dad shouted for him to stop and when he didn't, Dad ran after him. The event scared me. I didn't know why my dad would chase a man, but I assumed it was to punish him for going through our garbage. When Dad got back, I asked him if he caught the hobo and punished him. Dad said "No, Reggie. I ran after him because he didn't have anything to eat. I gave him five dollars." I knew that was the amount of spending money my dad allotted himself each week. It opened my heart and I never looked at people in need in the same way again. My dad felt empathy, and I could feel what my dad felt for the hobo.

Then of course, when the experience of not having money for food happened in my family that I described in the chapter on *Survive*, I was set up to understand the idea that people, through no fault of their own, may not have enough food to eat. I learned that there was a cushion in the form of food stamps and food pantries for families in that situation. I learned to value social programs meant to help people survive.

In my working life, the desire to care for others was expressed for a number of years in my work as a counselor and then as the Director of Social Work for Visiting Nurse Service and Hospice (VNSH). The job was both satisfying and fulfilling work for me. I visited with each patient and their caregivers, finding any gaps in care, and locating social service programs to address the gaps.

One of the social service programs we could provide to caregivers of Alzheimer's patients was a State funded program called Respite Care. A home health aid would go into the client's home for a few hours each week and take over the patient care. That allowed the caregiver to leave the house and do something alone for a while.

In this instance VNSH, the State's Respite Care Program, and my job are all expressions of *Care & Empathy*.

A Note About Burnout:

In *Care & Empathy*, our attention may extend only outward to others, and not extend inward to include ourselves. We may find ourselves working long hours, never finding enough time to address everyone else's needs and take care of ourselves too. This sets us up for burnout.

One Action to Take Today to Explore Consciousness:

Remember that in *Care & Empathy*, love equals caring for, taking care of, and feeling empathy for others. And fear equals the feeling that I can't take care of everyone who needs to be cared for.

Do an empathy experiment.

Think about a person you might feel sorry for—anyone at all—a homeless person or a friend, and imagine yourself in his or her shoes. Close your eyes and really put your full self into the experience. Imagine how the person feels. Imagine what their perspective on life might be. Imagine what their history might be.

Notice the difference inside of you between feeling sorry for someone and feeling empathy for the person.

Section Three

Integrate & Be Authentic, Be Oneness, and Be Creation

Making the shift from living predominantly in *Care & Empathy* to living in *Integrate & Be Authentic* (in any area of life) is nothing short of remarkable. I conceptualize this leap as something like a golden bridge that gets built over a chasm that had once been impassable. For some reason, we look at one part of our experience and whereas before we walk over the bridge, we see that piece of experience as isolated, on the other side of the bridge, we see the experience in all of its connections as part of a whole. When we make this leap in one part of life, before long, other parts of life move into being conceptualized as connected and part of the whole as well. I'll give examples of this in the next chapter.

Another feature that marks our thinking on the other side of the bridge, is that we move from a *subsistence existence* to *Being*. What does that mean? *Subsistence existence* means that our thinking minds are preoccupied much of the time with trying to be enough, have enough, care enough, work enough, and so on. *Being* means that our minds are no longer preoccupied with any of those thoughts. Instead, we know that we are enough, we have enough, we care enough, and we work enough. *Being* means that we are alive in the present moment much more often than not.

The third feature that is different on the *Being* side of the bridge is that we move quickly from empathy to compassion.

Thinking is non-dualistic—we have dropped the habitual mind pattern of categorizing and separating others (or anything at all), and easily cooperate with people expressing life from other facets of consciousness. Because of the felt sense of connectivity, we are able to support people where they are, not as a ponderous mental activity, but as a natural response in the moment. There is no longer one right way to do something because we see everything through a lens that understands each Iota of Being as one functioning part of Wholeness.

We'll be looking at specifics of what this means as we look at *Integrate & Be Authentic, Be Oneness, and Be Creation* in the next three chapters.

INTEGRATE & BE AUTHENTIC

Love and Fear

Love = Integration/connectivity/authenticity/ understands with the heart and the whole body/work with purpose.

Fear = Never takes action from fear. As soon as it's recognized, it is acknowledged, thanked, transmuted.

Keep in mind that…

Consciousness is a cloud of potential awareness, part of the unseen world that permeates all of the space and material of existence. We grow in consciousness in response to different conditions life presents to us and must consider how we'll respond. Will we respond from an internal position of love, or will we choose to react in fear?

When we're functioning primarily from *Integrate & Be Authentic*, we have thought deeply about our own beliefs and values, have integrated and live from them. They may or may not align with the beliefs and values of the culture in which we live. Living authentically, being true to our core Self is most important, so external pressure from a person or group does not sway us. We are principled. Our values are derived from the realization and *felt sense* of profound connectivity between all things—from the Wholeness of Life itself. We see Life and consciousness as an interconnected Whole and appreciate the strengths and skills we develop in every facet of consciousness.

We may feel fear, but as soon as we recognize it, we resolve and transmute[6] it. We aren't intimidated by complexity and not only are we not afraid of chaos we greet it as a creative tool and problem-solving partner. We are information gatherers and learners. We look for opportunities to learn from anyone and any experience, at any time. We're able to look at problems rationally and we have the ability to carry through with solutions, even when they take extended time and dedicated effort. We will gladly lead the work, but if someone else is better qualified and more knowledgeable, we are perfectly happy to follow her or his direction.

In *Integrate & Be Authentic,* we are likely to choose to live simply. We've eliminated the need to be anything other than ourselves—we no longer feel the need to put on a game face or send an artificially presented part of ourselves into any situation. We are enough.

One common experience we have which can introduce us to the connectivity of *Integrate & Be Authentic* might

---

[6] To transmute something means to change it from one thing into another. Tonglen is one of the ways to do this. Type "Tonglen meditation" into your web browser, and then click on a Youtube video. I like Pema Chodron's—it's very clear and easy to learn. Then simply do the practice with fear whenever you notice it welling up inside.

happen when we hold our baby for the first time. In many of us, the feeling wells up powerfully. We feel a physical sensation of warmth in the center of the chest, and an overwhelming connection of love.

Many of us have had the experience of thinking about someone and then the phone rings and it's the person we've been thinking about. Then we might think to ourselves, "that's weird," and discount it as a one-off. At some point we have enough of these that we begin to think about it as a larger experience of connection. We become aware that connectedness is our natural state—it's already there, always. Essentially, we wake up to that condition and begin living it.

My experience with Connectivity

One of the ways in which I experienced this natural state of connectivity was when I was in my early thirties and working on my second children's book. My first had been published the year before. It's out of print now, but its title was <u>Mary Regina's Secret Room</u>. The one I was working furiously on came to me in a dream. It was called *"Mary Regina and the Temple of the Magicians."* I couldn't get it down on paper fast enough, and worked on the drawings morning to night. I finished the book in one week.

At the end of the week, I got a call from my brother, who lives 3,000 miles away from me in San Francisco. This was before cell phones and personal computers became a ubiquitous part of life. The calls between us were made on landlines and were infrequent and expensive. My brother told me that he'd just gotten home from a trip to Mexico. He wanted especially to tell me about a Mayan ruin he visited. He said that the entire time he was there I was on his mind. It felt like I was right there with him, so much so that he took a photograph and was going to send it to me. He said the ruin was at a place called Uxmal, and it was specifically at the Temple of the Magicians that he thought about me non-stop.

That wigged me out! When I received the photograph from him a week later I couldn't believe my eyes. The structure I had drawn looked exactly like the photograph my brother sent to me!

I never submitted *"Mary Regina and the Temple of the Magicians"* for publication, however, the experience was so powerful that I began thinking about and researching connectivity. At the time I didn't realize that these experiences of connection were beginning forays into *Integrate & Be Authentic*. This is how it started for me. I began reading everything I could about how we are connected, and about connectivity in general. From Jane Addams' ideas about how we human beings comprise "organic wholes," to the secular writings of physicists, especially those of Einstein, Heisenberg, and Bohr.

Another foundational experience in connectivity for me happened about 20 years ago, but the story began when I was 18 years old. I was desperately in love, and in true teenage fashion, I knew this was the guy I'd be with forever. We had plans to get married. I got pregnant. He was just a teenager too and fell in love with someone else. I knew I'd have to give the baby up for adoption—I had no way to support a child by myself.

This was in 1967 and I went to live in a home for unwed mothers. My baby was born a little early and weighed just over five pounds. Because of that, I didn't get to hold her until the day I had to sign the adoption papers that released her to her adoptive parents. I got to hold her for about fifteen minutes. The memory of those moments still make me cry, feeling at the same time both gratitude and loss.

Fast-forward to about 20 years ago.

I was on an escalator in a mall going down when I saw her. I had held her for just those few minutes, thirty-plus years before, and I recognized my baby in the eyes of a woman who was riding the escalator in the opposite direction.

I wrote to her through the adoption agency. I told her a little about myself and asked her how her life had been. When she wrote back, she said that her life had been filled with so much love that it had a near fairy tale quality. She said she knew she was adopted and had always been curious about me. Because of that, when she was out in the world, she would look into the faces of people to see if anyone looked like her. She said that once when she was riding a mall escalator she saw a woman looking at her who looked like she had seen a ghost.

She realized she would look like that woman when she was older.

I think of that as an experience of extreme connectivity. It includes all aspects of Being: body, mind, heart, and Sprit. I now have experiences representing extreme connectivity every day, and often, they permeate the moments of my daily life.

One Action to Take Today to Explore Consciousness

Think about your own core values and write a list of your top ten. Think about how you are living your life, and whether your life and your core values are aligned. Now think about the values being expressed by the culture in which you are immersed. Notice the similarities and differences. Notice any pressure you may feel to "come into the fold" of the cultural values. Practice Tonglen with that pressure. Here is a brief description: Take a few deep breaths to quiet the mind, then inhale the feeling of pressure you're experiencing, and on the out breath, exhale peace or space into that pressure. Continue the practice whenever you feel that pressure. It will eventually dissolve completely.

BE ONENESS

Love and Fear

Love = Experience of Wholeness with all-that-is, including a felt sense of both the seen and unseen world.

Fear = Any disruption of Oneness. It is worked with as light in the immediate present, as a part of Oneness itself, and transmutation is lived experience in each moment—it is automatic.

Keep in mind that…

Consciousness is a cloud of potential
awareness, part of the unseen world that
permeates all of the space and material of
existence. We grow in consciousness in
response to different conditions life presents
to us and must consider how we'll respond.
Will we respond from an internal position of
love, or will we choose to react in fear?

"We're far from the shallow now." Lady Gaga

I begin this chapter with a quote from the song,
"Shallow," written by Lady Gaga, for good reason. This *Be
Oneness* facet of consciousness is described by poets and
songwriters, and is inhabited by mystics, sages, and
healers, fractals and harmonics. All of us everyday folks
inhabit this facet in moments, and perhaps in exquisitely
filled days we experience this felt sense of Wholeness. I'll
do my best to describe it, and we'll reach together to
understand from our hearts and intuition.

Living from *Be Oneness*, we are aware of Wholeness all the
time. This is a step into living the connectivity of life in the
continuous present moment, our intuition—knowledge
and reasoning that comes to us through the heart—is well
developed and it leads us.

Hopefully, as I describe Wholeness, we'll be able to keep the felt sense of Wholeness throughout. Here goes.

Wholeness is a profound living relationship with all of Life. Here are a few examples:

As a human being, I am made up of the cellular structure of all biological life and am one expression of the Wholeness of Biological Life—a biological lived expression of this Earth.

As a human being, I am one expression of the Wholeness of Spirit—a spiritual expression of Itself. As I become conscious of myself as Spirit, Spirit can know Itself through me.

As a human being, I am one expression of the Wholeness of Felt Sense Experience—an experiential expression of Felt Sense.

As a human being, I am one expression of the Wholeness of Love—an experiential expression of Love. As I become conscious of myself as Love, Love can know Itself through me.

As a human being, I am one expression of the Wholeness of Consciousness—a conscious expression of Consciousness. As I become conscious of that, Consciousness can know Itself through me.

As a human being, I am one expression of the Wholeness of Light—a shining expression of Light itself. As I become conscious of that, Light can know Itself through me.

As a human being, I am made up of the atoms and molecules that express themselves as both particles and waves, continuously connected with all atoms and molecules of Being in one expression of the Wholeness of All-That-Is. As I become conscious of Being an instance of expression of the Wholeness of All-That-Is, the Wholeness of All-That-Is can know Itself through me.

I could go on like this, ad infinitum, but I'm sure by now, you get the drift. Wholeness includes a lived relationship with everything in existence, so...

Living in *Be Oneness*, as I said earlier, means that we are led from the heart by our intuition and instinct, all of which is inseparable from our reasoning mind. Our conscious and subconscious mind works together to co-create life. Taking alone time is essential self-care. When we do that, we're able to expand our view of any specific thing—a person, experience, or event—to grasp the larger picture of which it is a part, in the moment. We take action to serve the good of the Whole and all its parts.

In *Be Oneness*, we view the Earth as a Whole/Gaia/a single Being/ecosystem, of which every existent life form, species, creature, and person is a part. We have a felt sense of energy fields, which may include sight, scent, or hearing, but is most often an intuitive felt sense. This quote from Buckminster Fuller is a good description of life lived through the lens of Wholeness.

"In short, physics has discovered

that there are no solids,

no continuous surfaces,

no straight lines;

only waves,

102

no things

only energy *event* complexes,

only behaviors,

only verbs,

only relationships..."[7]

Buckminster Fuller

Life is layered with the continuous experience of reverence—everything is viewed as Sacred. Everything. We are filled with wonder almost all the time. The ego is replaced with humility because of the continuous awareness that we are a lived expression of Wholeness. We are conscious, creative observers and participants in life.

Be Oneness Life Experience

I'm not a person who lives continuously from *Be Oneness*, but I do have a life experience to use as an example. It happens when I am painting or writing. This is a photograph of a recently finished painting.

---

[7] Fuller, R. Buckminster. *Intuition*. Impact Publishers, San Luis Obispo, CA, 2nd edition, 1983. Pg. 52.

"What Would Love Do (if the answer includes me)?"[8]

Regina Leffers, Oil on Canvas, 30"x30"

When I paint, I am so engaged in the work that I lose all track of time. I lose consciousness of myself as separate from the painting. I become one with the painting itself, the activity of painting, the oil paint, the brushes, the canvas, the space within which I am working, and life itself. When I emerge from the experience, it feels like I'm coming to the surface after swimming deeply. I begin to

---

[8] To view this painting in color, go to reginaleffers.com.

feel myself as a separate individual. After I've returned to the consciousness of imagined separateness, I often look at what I've painted and have no idea how it was done. I became consciously aware of having this experience forty years ago. It is the simple activity of being so engaged/present in the moment that I lose all track of time, separateness, and space.

Cheryl's Be Oneness Life Experience

Cheryl lives much of life from the inside of *Be Oneness* and has given me permission to document her experience. She is centered in living from Love most of the time and describes her experience like this.

> I move in to what I am seeing. I become it, and it becomes me. It doesn't matter what it is—it can be artwork, sandhill cranes flying high in the sky, a hawk or any soaring bird, even falling snow. I will be watching it, and then all of a sudden, I am the hawk soaring, circling, high overhead. I am the snow falling in huge, gentle flakes. My greatest pleasure is in being still, being wide open, being what is.

The other night when we were at an art exhibition called "Mother Sea," by artist, Sayaka Ganz, I had to back up and stand against the wall in order to stabilize as myself-in-the-art.

When people talk to me, I spread out and have to ask myself to draw back from the fullness of it to be able to focus in on the particulars of what is being said. I've learned that when my spouse and I go out to dinner, it is best if I can be facing the wall. When I do that, I have a better chance of remaining aware of the specific conversation we're having. If I'm facing out, I become the restaurant, the people in it, the cacophony of sounds, and I have to work hard to keep track of conversation at the table.

My feet are firmly planted in two worlds— the conscious and the subconscious—and I create life from that space. Sometimes I feel like I live my conscious life from a possibly stronger, more connected and more integrated subconscious Wholeness.

Solitude comforts, heals and fuels/ignites
me. Being alone helps me to become aware
of parts of myself that need forgiveness,
understanding, and compassion. I feel like I
reach back in time and heal old wounds
and hurts that have left scars. This activity
clears up any resentment that may be
hanging out in my subconscious mind.
Often, this process of transmuting old
wounds is not conscious, it just happens. It
feels like an opening into a deeper and
more expansive, compassionate sense of
myself.

Cheryl Spieth Gardner is a member of the Focus Group
for this book. Thank you for sharing your experience.

One Action to Take Today to Explore Consciousness

Remember moments when you were so completely absorbed by what you were doing that you lost all track of time and space, all sense that you were separate from what you were doing. Cultivate those moments.

BE CREATION

Love and Fear

Love = Experience of Creation. Feels everything—
every Iota of Being in its highest potential and
holds that as life itself. There is no difference
between the seen and unseen world—moves
between them as easily as life itself.

Fear = Does exist here, but because all of life is
experienced as one indivisible Whole, it is not felt
as separate from love. It is simply part of the
oscillation that exists in the experience of life.

> ## Keep in mind that…
>
> Consciousness is a cloud of potential
> awareness, part of the unseen world that
> permeates all of the space and material of
> existence. We grow in consciousness in
> response to different conditions life presents to
> us and must consider how we'll respond. Will
> we respond from an internal position of love,
> or will we choose to react in fear?

The Focus Group for this book decided to conduct an experiment. We wanted to know if we could expand our consciousness to this *Be Creation* facet of consciousness and stay aware of the physical body. We also wanted to know if we could describe the experience. We were to conduct the experiment on our own and report back the following week at our next meeting. The results were interesting.

In case you want to try it, the idea from Focus Group member, Calvin, is to imagine that just as water expands to fill all the space in a glass, we invite our consciousness to expand to fill all the space that is. If you have trouble allowing your consciousness to expand beyond the walls of the room or building you're in, imagine yourself first as the atoms and molecules that make up your physical being, then imagine the space between those atoms and molecules. Now imagine physicality itself as the space between atoms and molecules and invite your consciousness to expand to the edges of existence.

We found the *Be Creation* experience to have some common principles, (or perhaps beliefs) to consider.

Everything is Sacred. Everything.

We are in Relationship with this *Be Creation* facet of consciousness.

My part of the relationship is to be Intentional about opening to it.

There is no separation between what we think of as material/physical and what we think of as spiritual/unseen.

Be Creation speaks to me as more of a prompt. It asks me to think about my own consciousness—what am I taking in? And what am I sending out? And is that what I want to take in and send out?

The experience is one of Freedom and Stillness.

Here are some of the descriptions members of the Focus Group came up with.

"When I opened to *Be Creation*, I felt like I went into hyperspace. My body felt like it was hollow—just a shell. I could feel it, but couldn't move it. I didn't want to move or necessarily even be in the body. I wondered if *Be Creation* is where all of our Spirits meet. I felt no separation between anything. I felt the desire to honor and revere every single thing as Sacred."

"I felt stillness and calm—almost like a lack of experience. I felt the frequencies of sound energy. Booming and piercing— how everything unifies and cancels. I entered a thought process of simplifying all fundamental blocks/vibrations to their absolute essence. I found all the complexity we imbue in everything is hilarious when we see that it is all actually so simple. I realized that joy comes from harmonizing with the existing environment."

"My ego is aware of releasing any fear about there being no limits. I felt myself relax into the experience of no limits. The visual aid that came was that it was sort of like being a woman wearing hoop skirts and how difficult it is to navigate inside of a house, through doorways and around furniture. Then the woman is outside and there is no feeling of restriction of movement any longer — there is complete freedom. I felt the reality that I am larger than I believe I am, and that I am constantly being impacted by the world and that I am constantly impacting the world. I felt *Be Creation* as a prompt, asking me if what I am sending out is what I want to be sending out. It made me think of the practice of Tonglen."

"I felt that movement into *Be Creation* wasn't something that I did by myself. I opened to it and something larger—the unseen world/vibrations—draws to me. Most importantly, I felt myself in

relationship with it. I invite or intend and
it responds. I felt the reality that love and
fear are not separate. Instead they are like
one constant wave or oscillation—the in
and out of consciousness itself."

In the *Be Creation* facet of consciousness, the primary
experience we had is that everything is Sacred. And when
I am in Relationship with the Universe/All-that-Is through
the portal of Sacredness, nothing is separate. Life
experience is Wholeness Itself. I am wholly human,
connected and fully present in human form. I am scent. I
am music. I am Earth. I am the Cosmos. I am gravity and I
am light. I am the place where everything can be believed,
and also the place where nothing can be believed.

We also felt Love to be a state of Being. It is infinite and all
encompassing and radiates 360 degrees with zero specific
focus and zero barriers or limitations. The deeper and
more expansively we love and become love, not in what
we do but in who we are in each moment, we move into
this *Be Creation* facet of consciousness. Love is Spirit. The
more we enable ourselves to let go into love, to be and
embody love, the more we live Spirit in our physical
bodies.

We all had a difficult time putting our experience into

words. We marveled at and felt grateful for the poets of the world and their ability to describe experience that defies description. We talked about having to use words like "love" that already carry meaning that is diluted and limited when we put them to this use. We talked about having to use analogies as a temporary convenience to try to point to true experience, and the danger of doing so. The experience of the *Be Creation* facet of consciousness is radically different than anything we've experienced before. All metaphors come from past experience and because of that, are too shallow. They can't really convey the meaning we're trying to get at.

And one final thing to think about in the realm of *Be Creation...*

Calvin talked about the cochlea, the snail-shaped part of the ear that receives sound vibrations, and his thoughts about it resonated with the entire Focus Group. He talked about this piece of the body that has evolved to have stiffness at one end so that high frequencies stimulate it, and softness at the other end, enabling low frequencies to be received. These received vibrations get converted into nerve impulses, which can then get interpreted by the brain. The only thing the cochlea had to do was exist and the universe imprinted on it.

All we have to do is exist, and the universe imprints on us.

Maybe that leaves us with more questions than answers in this facet of consciousness, but we'll have to leave it at that. Experiment with *Be Creation* yourself. Repeat.

Appendix

Following are some useful methods of elevating the quality of our awareness, mindfulness, or Presence-in-the-moment.

Sutra Statements.

What are they and how can they help?

A sutra statement is equal to this combination: an *intention* plus a *prayer* plus an *affirmation* plus a feeling of *gratitude* plus an understanding of *right timing,* all wrapped into one.

Let's walk through the practice using one of the sutra statements I have worked with. The statement has been a transforming one for me. This is it: "I am completely unconnected to the good or bad opinions of others."

This is relevant for me because I have tried to please others all of my life, have tried to conform to the cultural rules describing "right behavior," and have made many life choices to fit in with those conventional ideas. Because those choices didn't reflect an authentic version of who I am, life got tied up in knots, and I've had to spend lots of valuable time untying them. Luckily, I've learned a lot in the process.

This is how I build a sutra statement into a daily practice by using the tools of *intention + prayer + affirmation + gratitude + right timing*. Even though I am separating them out for ease of explaining them, I work with these concepts all at the same time.

Working with the statement as if it were an *intention,* means that I quiet my mind, close my eyes and say to myself: "I am completely unconnected to the good or bad opinions of others." Then, I bring the image into my mind of this intention as a drop of water and I imagine dropping it into a still lake. I see the ripples of the drop expand outward in all directions. I watch the water return to calm on the surface as this intention gets absorbed into the body of water. With intentions, we speak them and let them go.

Working with the statement as if it were a *prayer,* means that I connect with God in a way that I feel that which is Sacred inside of me. Religions have different versions of God, and I'm going to share my version with you. I grew up in the Catholic religion, and all of the pictures of God to which I was exposed, were depictions of an older looking white guy wearing white robes, white hair, and white beard. In fact, Gandalf the Wizard from the movie, The Hobbit, looks a lot like the God of my childhood imagination.

My image of God has evolved through the years, of course. The current version consists of four parts. I described the first part in the Dedication of this book as a Presence that is profoundly interested in me (and in all of us, but I'm sticking with me here) such that this Presence can't wait to see what I'm going to do next. It feels like LOVE on steroids. The second part is from an image given to me during another profound meditation. The image is of God as a brilliant light (like a sun) shining out in all directions, and each ray of light, as it shines, is an expressed part of God as an incarnated iota of Being, me and you, trees and flowers, sun, moon, stars, and the entire Universe. The third part is Creativity expressed as an *impulse to flourish* inside of every iota of Being. As a very rough example, an acorn has within it all of the instructions necessary for it to grow into an oak tree, once it is able to root in soil. The impulse to flourish is expressed inside of these instructions and in the way that it will grow toward the sun. The fourth part I find inside of myself when I am appreciating the beauty of Epic Nature. I think of it as mindful appreciation—a form of myself being/reflecting back as a version of the aspect of

God that is Presence.

So, in working with the statement as a prayer, I infuse the moment with my own Presence, Light, Creativity, and Appreciation, aligning myself with all that is Sacred within me.

Working with the statement using the tools of *affirmation* mean that I say it aloud while looking into my own eyes in the mirror. I feel *grateful* for the understanding that this change is already taking place inside of me, and that it will be fully instantiated at *exactly the right time*.

What is meditation?

Why might it be important to develop it as a daily practice?

Meditation is the action of *continually* quieting the surface chatter in the mind. Take a look at the thoughts that go on in the mind—everything from grocery lists to grievance lists, from judgments about anyone or anything to tasks remaining undone (by you, your spouse, your colleague, your teenager, etc.). In general, our thoughts are unproductive habits of mind. They usually run along the same old groove, over and over again. Inspiration offering creative or original solutions to problems can't arise because there is no room for them. They get drowned out by chatter about the problem.

When folks first try meditation, they mostly think two things: the first is that it's hard, and the second is that they aren't doing it right. When we close our eyes, and begin expressing the effort to quiet the mind, all of a sudden we become aware of the incredible amount of chatter going on in there! It seems the harder we try, the louder the chatter becomes. This is exactly the work of meditation— noticing the thoughts that arise and bringing the focus back to the quiet.

Usually, it helps to focus the mind on something, like a word, or the inhalation and exhalation of our breathing, the light from a candle, or a feeling of peace or friendliness in your own heart center (the center of the chest). When we find ourselves thinking about anything, we literally move our mind back to whatever it is that we are using as a focus point.

Yes, it is hard.

The alternative is harder because it means that life will continue to be lived through us as a natural expression of our habitual thinking patterns. *Our free will evaporates when we live our lives from the chatter.*

And that brings us to why it is important to develop a daily practice of meditation. Simply put, we regain our free will, and gain access to more creative and novel ways to solve life's problems…whatever they are.

I'll be honest here. The chatter doesn't really ever stop. Sometimes we'll attain moments, minutes, even an hour or more of a quiet mind. But the action of meditation never changes. We just keep bringing the mind back to the meditative focal point whenever we discover the mind thinking about something.

I have been meditating everyday now for just over 40 years. I first learned to meditate in a group led by Conrad and Ilene Satala in Fort Wayne, Indiana and am very grateful for their excellent instruction—it is one of the things that changed the trajectory of my life. Developing a daily practice of meditation helped me gain access to my own creativity, a part of myself of which I had been unaware.

You don't need a group, and you don't have to have a live teacher to sit with. There are abundant resources available from which to learn. If you conduct a YouTube search on meditation, you'll get more than seven million results! I can't vouch for them, but I know you'll find a few on the very first page of results that can help you learn to meditate. There are also Apps for your phone that can give you an assist as well. I've tried most approaches to meditation over the years, and the best advice I can give is to choose one that feels right to you. There is no "one right way" to do it.

I learned the following version of a meditation practice at a retreat a few years ago. I sit comfortably with my back straight, feet flat on the floor, hands on my lap, and close my eyes. I ask myself the following questions slowly:

1. Who am I?
2. What do I want?
3. What is my purpose?
4. What am I grateful for?

I don't try to answer the questions. I simply notice any responses that might arise. Then I focus my mind at my own heart center and on the word, "Om." When a thought arises, I bring my attention back to the word, "Om." My meditation lasts for anywhere from 20 minutes to an hour, depending on the amount of time I have. Again, this is just one version—there is no "one right way" to meditate. Try this one out, and try a dozen others. The most important thing is consistency—meditate every day, even if you only have a few minutes to devote to the practice.

I learned to ask myself these questions at a Deepak Chopra retreat, "Seduction of Spirit," in April, 2017.

Love and Fear

At each stage of consciousness

Survive

Love = Feelings of security and safety. I have enough of what I need.

Fear = Feelings of insecurity and that there won't be enough. Once we've experienced not having enough of something, fear is always present in the background. It is most often experienced as an unnamed feeling in the gut.

Belong

Love = feelings of belonging and loyalty to the group.

Fear = the possibility of being cast out or shunned by the group. Fear is present in the background of consciousness if we have either expressed disloyalty to the group, or observed another member of the group being cast out.

Individuate

Love = the feeling of freedom and independence that comes with the action of individuating from our parents/family/ group.

Fear = the feeling of being dependent on and inability to be independent from our parents/family/group. This fear is nearly always in the background at this stage and looks like bravado.

Comply

Love = Is the feeling of loyalty to the family/group/culture—we want to learn its rules, and take them on as ours, because we want to feel connected in a way that goes beyond the feeling of belonging.

Fear = If I don't comply with the rules, I will disappoint them (my family, group, culture), won't be accepted by them anymore and will lose my connection to the group.

Re-individuate & Risk

Love = Feelings of empowerment, creativity, and the willingness to risk.

Fear = I might lose whatever it is that's important to me because I'm stepping away from what is acceptable to my family/group/culture.

Care & Integrate

Love expands to take the form of care and empathy.

Fear takes the form of feelings of being overwhelmed and inadequate.

Be Authentic

Love = authenticity/understands with the heart, the whole body/work with purpose

Fear = as soon as it's recognized, it is acknowledged, thanked, transmuted

Be Oneness

Love = Experience of Wholeness with all-that-is/seen and unseen world

Fear = felt as any disruption of Oneness/worked with as light in the immediate present, as a part of Oneness itself/transmutation is lived experience in each moment—it is automatic

Be Creation

Love = Experience of Creation. Feels everything—every Iota of Being, the highest potential and holds that as life itself. There is no difference between the seen and unseen world—moves between them easily as life itself.

Fear = Exists, but is felt as part of Creation, so there is no difference.

Regina Leffers, Ph.D.

My undergraduate degrees are in Psychology and Philosophy and I earned my doctoral degree in Philosophy from Purdue University. Creativity, Meditation, Sustainability, and Being Kind are what I aspire to and value most in myself.

Some of my favorite ways to express creativity are painting and writing. I have begun each day with meditation for 40+ years. Although I didn't know it at the time, this combination of studying Psychology + Philosophy + Meditation equals the study of Consciousness.

I am profoundly grateful for life as it is given to me in each moment.

Made in the USA
Middletown, DE
12 August 2019